A BIOGRAPHY OF JESUS

32 SIMPLE LESSONS FROM HIS LIFE

TOM J. COWLEY

ORDERED AROUND FOUR GEOGRAPHIC LOCATIONS OF CHRIST'S MINISTRY

NAZARETH	CAPERNAUM	JUDEA / PEREA	JERUSALEM
COME DOWN	COME FOLLOW	COME LIVE	COME HOME
From his birth through the beginning of his public ministry	The great Galilee ministry	After the Transfiguration until the Triumphal Entry	The most important week, the Passion to Pentecost
30 + 1 Years	1½ Years	6 Months	7 + 50 Days

PARACLETE PRESS
BREWSTER, MASSACHUSETTS

To my wife, Karen

For her encouragement in our partnership for life and our efforts to ensure that our children, their spouses, and our grandchildren know Jesus personally. May all of us grow in knowledge and relationship with Jesus.

2012 First Printing

A Biography of Jesus: 32 Simple Lessons from His Life

Copyright © 2012 by Tom J. Cowley

ISBN 978-1-61261-145-7

Library of Congress Cataloging-in-Publication Data

Cowley, Tom J.
   A biography of Jesus : 32 simple lessons from his life : ordered around four geographic locations of Christ's ministry / Tom J. Cowley.
      p. cm.
   ISBN 978-1-61261-145-7 (trade pbk.)
   1. Jesus Christ—Biography—Textbooks. I. Title.
   BT301.3.C69 2012
   232.9'01—dc23
   [B]   2012002062

10 9 8 7 6 5 4 3 2 1

Published by Paraclete Press
Brewster, Massachusetts
www.paracletepress.com
Printed in the United States of America

CONTENTS

THE "IN's" OF NAZARETH

God Among Us

THE "C's" OF CAPERNAUM

New Covenant

THE "D's" OF JUDEA / PEREA

Disciples Coached
and Divinity Declared

THE "T's" OF JERUSALEM

Passion Week and Resurrection of Jesus

ACKNOWLEDGMENTS

There are many people I wish to acknowledge for their help in making this work possible. My loving wife, Karen, deserves first mention for the long hours she has invested in reading draft materials, commenting on format improvements, and giving encouragement when I most needed staying power. Particular thanks go to my daughter, Allison de Laveaga, for her editing assistance and creative ideas. My son, John Cowley, established a website at www.tomjcowley.com. Robbie Collins, an artist friend, prepared map sketches used in the book. Jon Sweeney at Paraclete Press provided important counsel and guidance to shape this book into its current form.

During the Doctor of Ministry program at United Theological Seminary, Dr. Shane Andrus, Dr. Sande Herron, Dr. Bill Harris, Dr. Lawrence Wilkes, Dr. Shalom Renner, and Dr. Harold Hudson provided valued advice. The women of the Biblettes (a home Bible study in Marin County, California), Wally and Rita Osgood, Walt and Doris Leyes, Ed Pincusoff, Art Ammann, MD, and Bill Blatz all participated in pilot tests for my final paper. I am thankful to all those who have encouraged my ministry of bringing order to spiritual information.

INTRODUCTION

My journey toward writing this book began in 1988 when our pastor, Ray Johnston, challenged those attending the first service in January to read the Bible cover to cover in the upcoming year. I took Ray up on his challenge. Over the course of that year I began to see how pieces of the Bible fit together. I became excited about bringing "order" to my previously "disconnected" parts of spiritual information.

Since that time my ministry has been to help others better understand the basic framework and ministry of the life of Jesus Christ. My approach is to organize and order the information in the Bible to make learning, memorization, and recall as easy as possible.

Teaching and preaching in a number of church settings and constant spiritual dialog with old and new friends led me to the conclusion that all people need to know more about the life and works of Jesus Christ. We all need to know Jesus. The Bible, and the life of Jesus in particular, is the story of God's plan for living life. A framework of his life can assist us on life's journey and bring our world closer to joy and peace.

Bible scholars sometimes note that we have only forty-five days of the life of Christ in the Bible's four Gospels. From this material, I have chosen thirty-two key events told around four geographic locations of his ministry to help you get a handle on the biography of Jesus—his life and teachings.

This book advances a simple, basic *journey* theology. There is very little dogma or doctrine promoted—just the life of a divinely human man who changed human history.

Much is written today about the historical Jesus. A problem I have is that much of this material challenges his divine nature and omits many miracles he accomplished. As we draw close to the human Jesus, we must also honor and worship his divine nature. For this reason the "bookends" of *A Biography of Jesus* are events 1 and 2 ("In the Beginning Was the Word" and "Infant Birth") and events 31 and 32 ("Tomb Is Empty" and "Teach and Talk").

In events 1 and 2 we read of God's decision to send his Son with God's Word through the Virgin Mary. In event 31, the tomb is empty, and he has risen! Event 32 shares the guidance of the risen Christ to his followers. He calls us to employ the power of the Holy Spirit to *teach and talk*. We are challenged to be his witnesses in a world that needs *more* of Jesus. These four bookend events are the cornerstone faith events for those who follow Jesus.

A Biography of Jesus is written to help you to order, understand, and remember the life of Jesus. You will meet Jesus through the thirty-two selected key events in various settings, as you walk with him and feel his challenges, joys, and concerns.

This book is "events driven." Why should we focus on events? We live in an event-driven information age. Overviews or summaries are a part of our twenty-two-minute newscasts. Often our commentators are trying to pack twenty or more stories into brief sound bites. Politicians are scheduling photo opportunities to communicate messages. Organizations hire event planners to create themes. More in-depth coverage of subjects is always available to us, but we have adapted well to learning large amounts of material in smaller bites (or bytes).

We are constantly learning from events. How people behaved, what they said, and what they did lead to impressions. We draw values or truths about the lives and goals of people from events. By ordering the events in the life of Jesus in our minds, we can know him better and have a closer relationship with him.

As Rick Warren reminded us in *The Purpose-Driven Life*, we were "created to become like Christ." Jesus taught in the oral tradition: clearing temples, delivering sermons on mountainsides, eating in homes, performing miracles with impact, telling parables, and teaching through encounters with Jewish leaders. He wanted observers to take home and use his messages.

The thirty-two events of Christ's life presented in this book are grouped by each type of event. The three types of events are:

1. *a* GOD *event* An event that only God is big enough to pull off. Examples are God's decision in heaven to send his Son, the Virgin Birth, and Jesus's resurrection.

2. *an* IMPACT *event* An event that had great impact and created an impression on observers. Examples are miracles, healings, and clearing the Temple.

3. *a* TEACHING *event* Jesus as seen teaching in the oral tradition, using parables, conversing over meals, preaching, and so on. Some of the sermons of Jesus, his close dialog with disciples, and the private time Jesus spent coaching his disciples are examples of teaching events.

Three more important concepts shape this guide and are designed to further enhance your ability to remember this material quickly and easily. These are additional "handles" for your study:

1. Four basic geographic locations provide order and chronology to Jesus's life.

The "four locations" approach to the life of Jesus started while I was facilitating a group pilgrimage to Israel in 1998. On that trip our group traveled throughout the entire Holy Land. The area in which Jesus ministered is about 150 miles long and 50 miles wide. In my own attempt to process all of the information, during the trip I observed that Jesus's ministry focused around four basic geographic areas. Three of these four locations are cities:

- Nazareth (his early years through age thirty-one)
- Capernaum (the one-and-a-half-year great Galilee ministry); and
- Jerusalem (Passion Week).

The fourth location encompasses two provinces:

- Judea and Perea.

These provinces are divided by the Jordan River; I have named them (rather than cities) because Jesus and his disciples were constantly traveling from city to city in Judea and Perea. The group was on the move for a six-month period from his Transfiguration to the triumphal entry into Jerusalem for Passion Week.

These four "base camps" of Jesus's ministry provide an overall chronological grouping of events in the life of Jesus. This is unique in relation to other more academic works I have studied; however, it is a concept that I find many people can relate to. Base locations are associated with major moves in our own lives as we change careers, move across country, or go through other major life changes.

2. Memory theory helps us recall events to deepen our learning and reflection.

God has created us with a marvelous memory capability, which often goes untapped. The human brain has the capacity for ten trillion bits of information. How do we store and recall those facts? One way is by focusing our attention on *stories* or *narratives*. Most people can remember a story better than a random set of facts.

To assist in this, the thirty-two key events of Jesus's life in this book are "chunked" around the basic locations of Jesus's life using alliterations in the titles. You saw these first on the contents page, where each title within the four sections begins with the same letter. These alliterations are designed to further help you in retaining the information of his biography. You may wish to develop your own additional word associations or visualizations for even greater recall. That is great! Use your mind to know Jesus better, retain key events, live his teachings, and share his biography.

3. The four locations of the ministry of Jesus open up the basics of Christian theology.

I remember once when Dr. Leonard Sweet delivered a sermon on the "Hour of Power" television service from the Crystal Cathedral Ministries. He shared a six-word simple theology: "Come Down, Come Out, and Come Home." With his kind permission, I have adapted Dr. Sweet's "simple theology" to eight words that are tied to the thirty-two events in this guide. They present a journey for us to discover and easily unpack the basics of Christian theology.

PLACE	SIMPLE THEOLOGY
Nazareth	Come down
Capernaum	Come follow
Judea/Perea	Come live
Jerusalem	Come home

You will find more on these four phrases of "journey theology" as the book progresses.

As you walk through the Gospels with me, focusing on thirty-two essential events in the life of Christ, I hope you will come to understand this journey theology more deeply. Jesus came not only to save us but to help us develop purpose on life's journey. We are all invited by him to:

Come down
Come follow
Come live
and Come home.

For those who have not yet chosen to follow Jesus, my purpose in *A Biography of Jesus* is to provide an opportunity to read his life as a sequence of memorable events. Don't rely on what others have said; study his life, teachings, and claims on your own. Consider the decision to follow him, based upon study of his life. For those who have already made a decision to follow Jesus, I pray this guide will deepen your relationship, love, and friendship.

COME DOWN

NAZARETH

From his birth

through the

beginning of his

public ministry

30 + 1 Years

7 Events

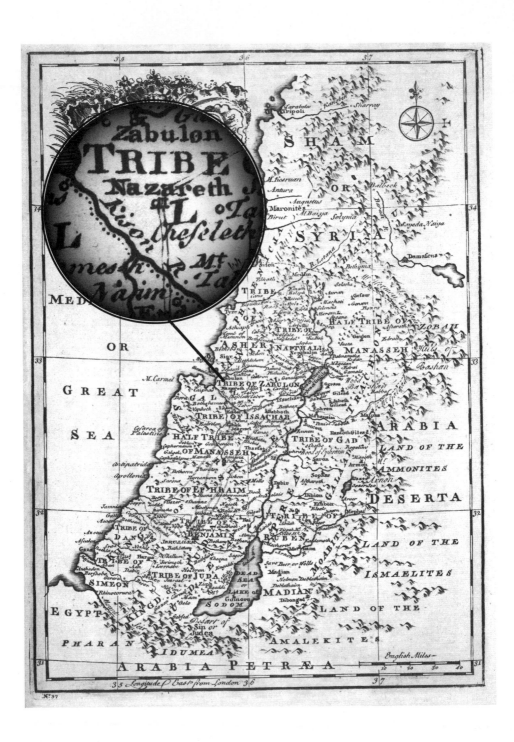

INTRODUCTION

NAZARETH is a city on a hill in Galilee. It overlooks the Jezreel Valley described in the Old Testament. Looking to the south on a clear day from Nazareth, you can see mounts Tabor, Moreh, and Gilboa. The village of Nain is also visible in the distance. Today Nazareth is primarily an industrial town housing an important automotive assembly plant. It is Israeli-occupied territory and has a large Arab (Islamic) influence.

Mary and Joseph journeyed from Nazareth to Bethlehem for the Roman imperial census when Jesus was born. They returned to Nazareth, after a brief stay in Egypt, to Joseph's carpentry business. As Matthew (2:23) notes, Jesus was called a Nazarene. Just as each of us has a hometown where we were brought up, Jesus could call Nazareth his hometown. It is interesting that the word *Nazarene* in Jesus's day was a synonym for "despised."

The seven events identified around Nazareth cover the longest period in his life, thirty-one years. IN's help us remember this first part of his life. For example, there was no room in the "Inn," and the baby Jesus was born in a humble Bethlehem stable, south of Jerusalem.

Of the seven events in this section, two are God events, four are impact events, and there is one teaching event. They are presented in chronological order.

Come Down

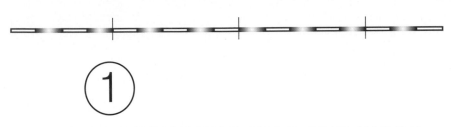

IN THE BEGINNING WAS THE WORD

a GOD *event*

God made the decision in heaven to send his Son, Jesus, to earth with his Word for living.

GOD, since creation, had interest in sharing his Word with his people. Moses conveyed God's law, the Ten Commandments, on Mount Sinai, but the Hebrew nation had trouble understanding and observing God's law. God decided on a different plan to share his Word, or Logos. He would send his son, Jesus, with the New Covenant for people. "The Word became flesh and made his dwelling among us" (John 1:14a). John affirms the divine (yet fully human) nature of Jesus.

Later the apostle Paul says, "But when the time had fully come, God sent his Son" (Galatians 4:4a). Hellenistic culture

(common Greek language and philosophy) and Roman advancements (transportation progress and roads) provided the "backdrop" for God to *fulfill* his promised Messiah. Think of the celebration in heaven! God had decided the fullness of time had arrived! God would send his Son with the Word. What is known as the Messianic Age begins with the coming of Jesus to the earth.

The Word (Logos) was to be fully human and dwell among us. God must have been disappointed that centuries of working with his chosen people, the Hebrews, had not produced much fruit. So he decided that the time had come for his Son, Jesus, to become flesh and dwell among people to share his Word.

The importance of proclaiming this Good News that God's Word came from heaven to visit the earth is still vitally important for our lives today.

Refer to: *John 1:1-18*

Question: If you were God and frustrated with centuries of trying to have your message for humankind communicated, what would you have done to secure the attention of people?

2

INFANT BIRTH

a GOD *event*

Through the Holy Spirit, the Virgin Mary conceives a Son.

I N this second event—clearly another "God Event"—we celebrate God's gift of light to the world each Christmas season. At the time that Herod was king in Judea, an elderly priest, Zechariah, and his wife, Elizabeth, conceived a son. Their son became John the Baptist. Meanwhile in Nazareth, the angel Gabriel visited Elizabeth's much younger cousin, Mary, and told her that she would bear a son who would be named Jesus, Son of God most high. Although Mary at first questioned Gabriel because she was a virgin and her betrothed, Joseph, gave thought to stepping quietly away from his engagement, both Mary and Joseph were obedient and became servants of the Lord.

During this time the Emperor Augustus decreed that a census should be taken. Mary and Joseph made their way from Nazareth to Bethlehem (the city of King David's birth). While she was there, Mary gave birth to the infant in a stable. Shepherds from the local fields and wise men from the East came to honor his birth. Matthew records the gifts of these wise men: *gold*, symbolizing royalty, a messianic king; *frankincense*, an ingredient in incense used for worship; and *myrrh*, another resin used to heal.

After eight days had passed the child, Jesus, was presented at the Temple in Jerusalem. Simeon, a righteous and devout man guided by the Spirit, blessed the Messiah. Soon Joseph was visited in a dream by an angel of the Lord. He was advised to flee with the child and his mother to Egypt and remain there until told otherwise. Desperate to protect his throne, Herod had ordered the slaughter of all male babies less than two years old in Bethlehem. Upon Herod's death, an angel appeared to Joseph ordering the return of his family. Fearing life in Judea, Joseph settled in his hometown, Nazareth.

Refer to: *Matthew 1:18–2:23*
Luke 1:5–2:40

Question: Can the God who created our vast universe orchestrate an impregnation and thus Virgin Birth in Mary?

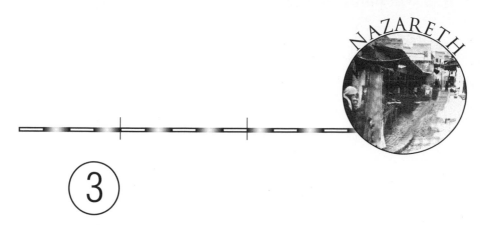

3

INCREASE IN WISDOM AND STATURE

an IMPACT event

Jesus visits the Temple in Jerusalem at age twelve and engages in spiritual dialog with teachers.

LITTLE IS KNOWN of the childhood of Jesus except for a Passover visit to Jerusalem when Jesus was twelve years old. In Luke 2:39 we are told Mary and Joseph did all required by the Law so that the child Jesus was filled with wisdom and the grace of God was upon him.

When Jesus visited the Temple in Jerusalem at age twelve, those who were within were amazed at his answers to their questions. We are told that he was about his Father's work in his house. Luke 2:52 adds, "And Jesus grew in wisdom and stature, and in favor with God and men." *Even Jesus could increase in wisdom and stature!*

Jesus must have been diligent in his study of the Old Testament Scriptures. He was delighted to be in his Father's house and dialog with teachers in the Temple courts. Spiritual dialog is an important part of a growing faith. Growing in wisdom and stature is a patient, maturing process in life.

Refer to: *Luke 2:41-52*

Questions: Was Jesus well trained in Hebrew Scripture and spiritual information by his parents? How could we better train our children in the Scriptures today?

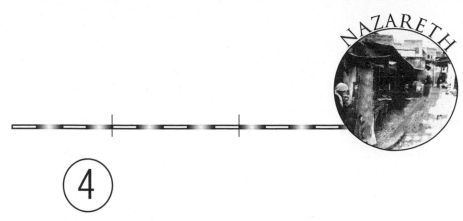

4

INSPIRATION OF JESUS

an IMPACT event

The baptism of Jesus marks the beginning of his ministry.

O N THE MEDITERRANEAN SCENE, it was the fifteenth year of the reign of Emperor Tiberius. Pontius Pilate was governor of Judea and Herod was ruler in Galilee. A word from God came to John, known as the Baptist, that he was to minister in the wilderness of the Jordan River.

Inspiration has a beginning. Age thirty was considered the age at which manhood began in the Hebrew community. Jesus, age thirty, was listening to God. He was inspired to leave a carpentry business and fulfill a calling from God. Jesus comes to the River Jordan and is baptized by John. A voice came from heaven: "You are my Son, whom I love; with you I am well pleased" (Luke 3:22b).

It must have been important that Jesus knew his Father loved him and was pleased with him. As his ministry began, Jesus also must have felt John's affirmation. John said, "After me will come one more powerful than I, the thongs of whose sandals I am not worthy to stoop down and untie. I baptize you with water, but he will baptize you with the Holy Spirit" (Mark 1:7–8).

Also, affirmation in our lives is important. When we hear or sense a calling or undertake a task, it is important to recognize that the Holy Spirit is at work in our lives.

Refer to: *Matthew 3:1–17*

Mark 1:1–11

Luke 3:1–22

John 1:19–34 and *3:22–36*

Questions: How were the timing and the setting right for this key transition event, or marker, in the life of Jesus? Are there markers and transitions you can recall in your own life?

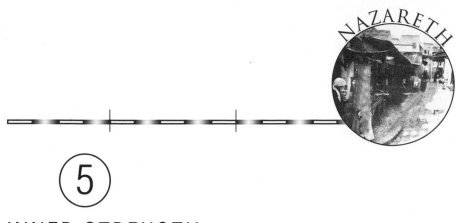

5

INNER STRENGTH

a TEACHING *event*

Jesus teaches us about temptation and the wilderness.

THE SPIRIT led Jesus to fast in the wilderness on his journey to Jerusalem. He was tempted for forty days. After we receive inspiration and affirmation to serve the Lord, the temptation of worldly pleasures and other commitments always seem to enter our lives.

Matthew in chapter four records how Jesus faced three temptations and answered each one with God's Word from the Old Testament (Deuteronomy 8:3b, 6:16a, and 6:13a).

DEVIL'S TEMPTATIONS	JESUS'S ANSWERS
Turn stones to loaves of bread.	Man does not live on bread alone, but by every word that comes from the mouth of the Lord.
If you are God, jump from the pinnacle of the Temple—safely.	Do not test the Lord your God.
Bow down and worship me and I will give you material splendor.	Fear the Lord your God, serve him only.

We can all identify with temptations—even some of these.

Refer to: *Matthew 4:1-11, Mark 1:12-13,*
Luke 4:1-13
Related readings: *Deuteronomy 6:13, 6:16,*
and 8:3

Questions: Do temptations keep you from following Christ?
How do you face them?

INITIAL ENCOUNTERS

IMPACT *events*

Jesus has impact on Nicodemus, people at a wedding, Temple leaders, a woman at a well, and others.

HERE WE SEE JESUS starting his ministry after his baptism showing great inner strength after overcoming temptation in the desert. These next events of Jesus's first year of ministry flow quickly. The Gospel of John records them as follows:

- Jesus calls his first disciples.

- He changes water to wine at a wedding in Cana.

- He clears the Temple in Jerusalem of money changers.

- He encounters the Pharisee Nicodemus by night and advises him that he must be born again.

- He meets a Samaritan woman at a Sychar well and converts her to become the first evangelist for his ministry.

- He heals a nobleman's son.

Each of these encounters shows a fully human, loving Jesus in the beginning of his ministry. Meanwhile they show Jesus making friends, enjoying a wedding, showing love for people, telling important truths, being open to all including a Samaritan woman, and healing a faith-filled official's son.

Refer to: *John 1:35–3:21* and *4:1–54*

Questions: Can you see any common features in these initial encounters? What do these early events in Jesus's public ministry tell you about his purpose, his intentions?

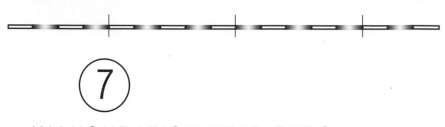

7

INAUGURATION YEAR ENDS

an IMPACT *event*

Rejection in Nazareth causes Jesus to move his ministry to
Capernaum.

IN THIS LAST EVENT from the Nazareth period, we
see Jesus reading from scrolls of Isaiah in the synagogue
of Nazareth. He announces that the Lord has anointed
him to preach the good news to the poor, proclaim freedom
for prisoners, recover sight for the blind, and release the
oppressed. Jesus also proclaims that he is the fulfillment of the
Isaiah Scriptures. He predicts that no prophet will be accepted
in his hometown. The local people of Nazareth were furious
when they heard these things and drove him out of town!

The first year of Jesus's ministry, known as the year of
Inauguration, ends with rejection. As a result, he moves his

ministry to Capernaum, on the nearby shores of the Sea of Galilee. There, Jesus will begin what is known as the great Galilean ministry. He responded to rejection and the ending of his first year of public ministry in Nazareth by moving forward with God's call to him.

Refer to: *Luke 4:14-30*

Questions: How do you see Jesus handling rejection? Are there areas of your life where you could learn from this example, where you may need to move on to new challenges?

COME
FOLLOW

CAPERNAUM

The great

Galilee

ministry

1½ Years

10 Events

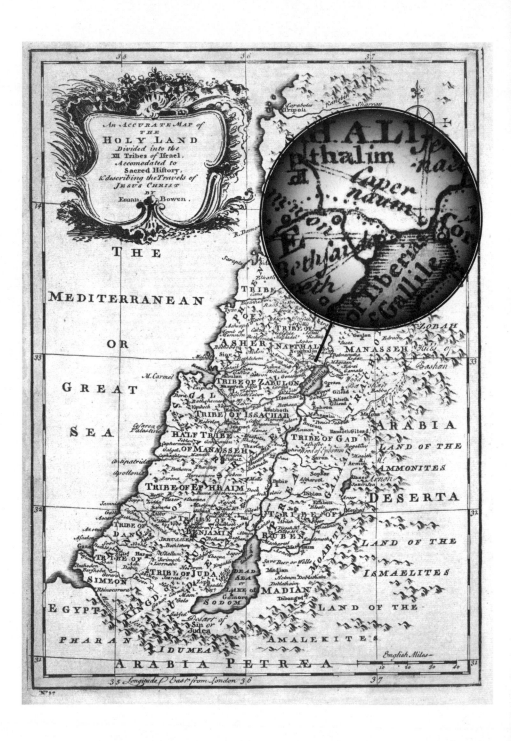

INTRODUCTION

After rejection in his local Nazareth synagogue, Jesus moved his ministry for the next one-and-a-half years to **CAPERNAUM**, on the Sea of Galilee. There Jesus emphasized the important teaching of the New Covenant in his ministry. Galilee proved to be a most responsive audience to his messages.

Simon Peter's home in Capernaum was the base in Galilee for Jesus and his travels. Jesus must have felt comfortable in the midst of these affirming surroundings. Fishermen, a tax collector, a Zealot, and people from all walks of a more rural life listened to his teachings. Hillsides beside the sea often provided natural amphitheater settings for his preaching and teaching. Some scholars refer to the time of Jesus in Galilee as the "Year of Popularity." Jesus was fully human (and fully divine) and must have felt good to be affirmed. We all like to be liked!

Much of our record of Jesus's ministry in Galilee comes from two Gospel writers: Matthew and Mark. Matthew, writing to Hebrews, wanted his listeners to understand a restatement of Hebrew laws and traditions. Mark, writing to Romans, emphasized Jesus's actions, miracles, and accomplishments.

Events referenced in Capernaum are ordered around ten C's to help recall the New Covenant. There are seven teaching events and three impact events. The individual Galilee events are *not* chronological; Matthew was guided by the principle of association. In all, God's laws are presented as ways of love, and we see living in the kingdom of God as lasting, compared to more earthly values.

Come Follow

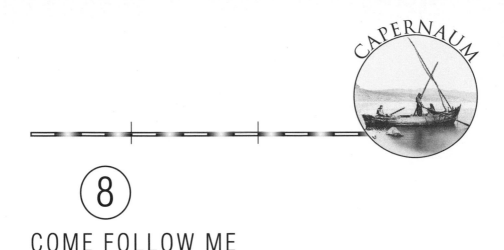

(8)

COME FOLLOW ME

an IMPACT event

Jesus calls his disciples to follow him and learn God's Word
for living.

AS JESUS MOVED HIS MINISTRY TO GALILEE, he began to gather disciples. Jesus called four common fishermen to "Come follow me, and I will make you fishers of men" (Matthew 4:19). The men, two sets of brothers (Andrew and Simon [Peter]; and James and John, sons of Zebedee), were engaged in successful fishing businesses on the Sea of Galilee. They immediately left their nets, answered his call, and became among his first disciples. This would mean leaving their emphasis on worldly matters for the values of God's kingdom instead.

Jesus encountered Levi (to be called Matthew) sitting at his tax booth. Jesus said to him, "Follow me," and Levi got up, left everything, and followed him. Following prayer with his Father on a mountainside, Jesus eventually called twelve disciples in all to be his close followers and companions (Luke 6:12–16). In Galilee many others joined the ministry and followed him as well. Not all who followed stayed with him for the long haul (John 6:60–71).

Refer to: *Matthew 4:12–25, 9:9–13*

Luke 6:12–16

Related Readings: *Mark 1:14–20, 2:13–17,* and

3:13–19

Luke 5:1–11 and *5:27–31*

John 1:35–51 and *6:60–71*

Questions: What do you think it means to be a fisher of men? Was that something only for Jesus and his disciples to do, or does it have relevance for us today?

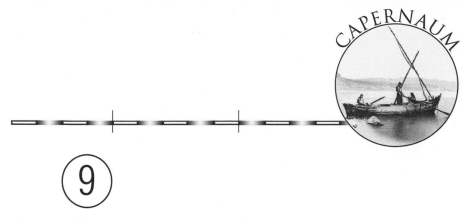

CAPERNAUM

9

CHANGED ATTITUDES

a TEACHING *event*

Sermon on the Mount (Part 1)

THIS IS THE BEGINNING of what is perhaps the greatest teaching event of all for Jesus, in which he suggests as a first step that his followers change their attitudes. In these teachings, problems and challenges become blessings—attitudes of God's kingdom, so to speak—rather than reasons to become bogged down by the world. These teachings are often referred to as the Beatitudes.

The nine attitudes of God's kingdom can be organized in many ways. One approach is to order the first four as an *inward* journey, leading to blessings of mind. The next four are an *outward* journey, providing blessings to others. Then the ninth is a capstone attitude about what it means to be blessed by walking in faith.

ATTITUDE	BLESSING THAT FAITH PROVIDES
Inward	
Poor in spirit	Theirs is kingdom of heaven
Mourn	They will be comforted
Meek	They will inherit the earth
Thirst for righteousness	They will be filled
Outward	
Merciful	They will be shown mercy
Pure in heart	They will see God
Peacemakers	They are called children of God
Persecuted for my sake	Theirs will be the kingdom of heaven

Capstone

"Blessed are you when people insult you, persecute you and falsely say all kinds of evil against you because of me. Rejoice and be glad, because great is your reward in heaven, for in the same way they persecuted the prophets who were before you" (Matthew 5:11–12).

Refer to: *Matthew 5:1-16*
Luke 6:17-26

Questions: Why do you think Jesus begins his teachings with these Beatitudes? Do these humbling attitudes make sense for us today?

(10)

COMMANDMENTS OF LOVE

a TEACHING *event*

Sermon on the Mount (Part 2)

THERE ARE MANY WAYS to order the Sermon on the Mount and the lessons for life Jesus shared. One way is this: after the opening Beatitudes, the Sermon divides into two parts: teachings about love for neighbor and teachings about love for God. This division reflects Jesus's greatest commandment when he summarized the law into loving the Lord and loving your neighbor (Matthew 22:37–39). We will consider the "love your neighbor" teachings first.

Jesus teaches a new form of love for this world: agape love. Agape love is learning to intelligently and intensely will the best for another. Agape is a love that expects nothing in return.

To love your neighbor in this way (according to Matthew 5:17–48) includes:

- Avoiding anger, for a sharp tongue can "murder."

- Refraining from lust, which leads to many troubles in relationships.

- Valuing marriage, godly love that does not encourage divorce.

- Keeping oaths; letting your "yes" be "yes" and your "no," "no."

- Turning the other cheek to those who attack you.

- Learning to love your enemies.

The Sermon on the Mount sets a high standard for followers of Jesus. He builds on the foundation of the Old Testament and the laws of Moses. As the prophet Jeremiah said: "'The time is coming,' declares the LORD, 'when I will make a new covenant with the house of Israel and the house of Judah'" (Jeremiah 31:31). "I will put my law in their minds and write it on their hearts" (Jeremiah 31:33b).

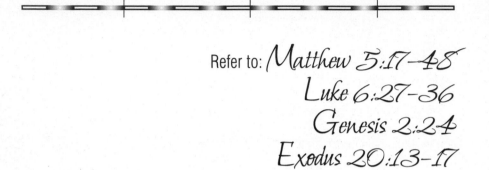

Refer to: *Matthew 5:17–48*
Luke 6:27–36
Genesis 2:24
Exodus 20:13–17

Questions: Do you think it is harder to follow the laws of the Ten Commandments or the two-part law summary of the New Covenant? What would a relationship built on agape love look like?

CAPERNAUM

CONSTRUCTION ON THE ROCK

a TEACHING *event*

Sermon on the Mount (Part 3)

JESUS concludes the Sermon on the Mount by stating that whoever hears his words and puts them into practice is a wise builder, constructing on rock. He outlines ways in which we can love God in Matthew 6 and 7.

WAYS TO LOVE GOD (Matthew 6–7)

- Give quietly to the needy.

- Pray to the Father the Lord's Prayer in private.

- Fast privately, don't look somber.

- Store treasures in heaven rather than on earth.

- Trust God, do not worry about tomorrow.

- Do not judge, trust God to judge.

- Make your needs known to God.

- Enter through God's narrow gate to life.

- Bear good fruit, like a godly tree.

- Build on solid rock, love God.

God desires that we love only him, serving obediently. Jesus calls us to build an indwelling temple, with himself as the cornerstone.

Refer to: *Matthew 6:1-7:29*
Related readings: *Luke 6:37-49, 11:2-4,*
and *12:22-34*

Questions: What do you think of the sequence Jesus established for loving God? Is it a good outline for people to follow in building their life?

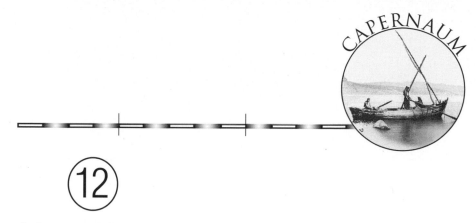

12

COMPASSION, CARING, CURING

IMPACT *events*

Healings and miracles of Jesus impact people.

T HE BIBLE (according to the *NIV Study Bible*) records a total of thirty-five miracles of Jesus. These miracles are recorded in all four Gospels (Matthew has twenty, Mark eighteen, Luke twenty, and John eight miracles). The majority, twenty-three of them, occurred during his ministry in Galilee. The *compassion* of Jesus can be noted as he accomplishes these miracles of *caring* and *curing*. In all, one senses the warm heart he had for people.

Here is a partial list of the twenty-three miracles showing Jesus's compassion. Seventeen involved healings and six showed power over nature. The events impacted crowds, brought attention to Jesus, and indicated his power and teachings.

EVENT	PASSAGE
Changes water to wine	John 2:1–11
Heals a man with leprosy	Mark 1:40–45
Heals the centurion's servant	Matthew 8:5–13
Heals two demon-possessed men	Mark 5:1–15
Arise and walk, a paralytic man is healed!	Mark 2:1–12
Heals on the Sabbath; Jewish leaders upset	John 12:1–14
Casts out demons	Luke 11:14–28
Calms storm and disciples' fears	Mark 4:35–41
Heals crippled woman on the Sabbath	Luke 13:10–17
Heals Jarius's daughter	Matthew 9:18–19, 23–25
Heals a bleeding woman	Matthew 9:20–22
Heals widow's son from death	Luke 7:11–17
Feeding of the 5,000	Mark 6:30–44
Walks on water	Matthew 14:22–33
Comforts a Greek woman	Mark 7:24–30
Heals a deaf mute	Mark 7:31–33
Feeding of the 4,000	Mark 8:1–13

Heals a blind man at Bethsaida	Mark 8:22–26
Heals a boy possessed by a demon	Mark 9:14–32
Heals infirm man at Sheep Gate pool	John 5:1–15
Restores sight to the blind	John 9:1–12
Raises Lazarus from dead	John 11:1–44
Withers a fig tree to represent dead faith	Matthew 21:18–22

Refer to: *Matthew*, *Mark*, *Luke*, and *John*

Questions: Look closely at two or three of these miracle stories. What do they have in common? How are they different from each other?

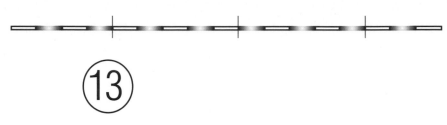

CENTRIFUGAL VERSUS CENTRIPETAL FAITH

a TEACHING *event*

Jesus sends disciples and John confirms his ministry.

JESUS made his promise of wholeness not only to his disciples, but to all those who decide to follow him. Wholeness can be viewed as discovering the unique person God wants each of us to become. In Matthew chapters 8–15 we observe Jesus bringing wholeness to those who believed. A part of wholeness is sharing our faith with others. He trained disciples to go out (*centrifugal*), two by two.

Jesus reminds his disciples, "The harvest is plentiful but the workers are few" (Matthew 9:37b).

In contrast, the Jewish faith had an inward focus (*centripetal*). Birth within a Hebrew family blood line was valued as a

key to full membership. Samaritans, for example, born to Jewish-Syrian families, were looked down upon. In Matthew 10 Jesus sends out his disciples to the lost sheep of Israel to share his message. Later, in final instructions to those who were about to become apostles of the faith, he expands the mission for his message to the ends of the earth (Acts 1:8). Jesus clearly envisioned a *centrifugal* faith for all the peoples of the world.

Meanwhile, John the Baptist, while in prison (Matthew 11), sends disciples to *confirm* the ministry of Jesus. The disciples find a valid ministry of healing and teaching. Jesus also affirms the greatness of John the Baptist in God's kingdom. Today, those serving Jesus need their ministries *confirmed* by thoughtful observers. This ensures that we are serving his kingdom.

Refer to: *Matthew 9–11*

Questions: Is it tempting to have a faith that is only centripetal? What are signs of an authentic ministry for Jesus today?

CULTIVATION OF THE WORD

a TEACHING *event*

Cultivating God's Word and remaining clean within.

IN MATTHEW 13, Jesus shares parables describing the kingdom of heaven. We hear a story of a farmer sowing seeds to illustrate the process of how we receive the Word of God. Some seeds fell on the path and were eaten by birds, never reaching the hardened human heart. Other seeds fell among the rocks, sprang up briefly before the sun parched the shallow soil, and are an example of those who listened to and observed only briefly, his teachings. Some seeds fell among the thorns and were choked as they grew. The Word is choked when we pursue both worldly and heavenly teachings. Finally, some seed fell on good soil, representing the fertile mind of a follower of Christ and his teachings. These seeds produced a crop that multiplied a hundred, sixty, thirty times what was sown!

Walking with Christ, cultivating and nurturing his teachings, produces a life of multiplication. Jesus shares other parables in Matthew 13. He describes the kingdom of heaven and highlights its values:

PARABLE	MATTHEW PASSAGE
Weeds, and good seed	13:24–30, 36–43
Mustard seed great among herbs	13:31–32
Yeast produces leaven	13:33–35
Hidden treasure, sells all he has	13:44
Fine pearls, of great value	13:45–46
Net to separate kinds of fish	13:47–52

In Matthew 15, Jesus teaches about what is "clean and unclean." He surprises those who expected him, rabbi that he was, to simply repeat the Old Testament laws on this topic. Instead, Jesus tells us that what comes out of our mouths is what is in our hearts—and *that* makes us clean or unclean (Matthew 15:1–20).

Refer to: *Matthew 13* and *15:1–20*
Mark 4:1–32 and *7:1–23*
Luke 8:4–18 and *13:18–21*

Questions: What does it mean to live a life of multiplication?
What are the "seeds" in your life?

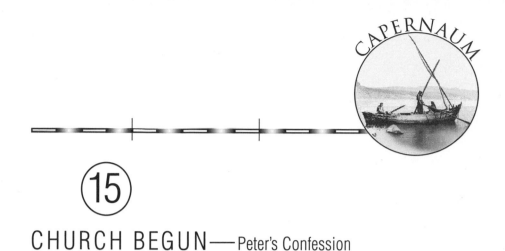

(15)

CHURCH BEGUN—Peter's Confession

a TEACHING *event*

Jesus, favorably disposed by Peter's affirmation, teaches what his church would be built upon, believers.

AS THE GREAT GALILEAN MINISTRY draws to a close, Jesus visits the region of Caesarea Philippi, a stronghold of Hellenistic thinking and worship of the Greek god Pan. It was here that Jesus asked Peter, "Who do you say I am?" "Simon Peter answered, 'You are the Christ, the Son of the living God.'" Jesus then states, "I tell you that you are Peter, and on this rock I will build my church, and the gates of Hades will not overcome it" (Matthew 16:16–19).

Jesus talks about building his church, or *ecclesia* in the original Greek, which means "called-out ones." We are the called-out ones, a community of believers.

In Matthew 18, Jesus then outlines a healthy church. He promises, "For where two or three come together in my name, there am I with them" (Matthew 18:20). As communities of believers, we all must look to his presence for health within the body.

The church may be viewed as a mission station, a place where believers come and are renewed in the spirit to fulfill their calling to serve Jesus Christ. I like to think of this as a church without doors, where a community of believers is prepared to go and lead a purpose-driven life. The community of believers is a place where doctrine and dogma take a back seat to a personal relationship with Jesus, a desire to see his teachings practiced in the world, and the fulfillment in daily life of that divine encounter.

Refer to: *Matthew 16:13–20* and *18:1–20*

Related readings: *Mark 8:27–30*

Luke 9:18–27

Questions: In what spiritual communities do you participate? Is it possible to be a follower of Jesus without being a part of a church or community of believers?

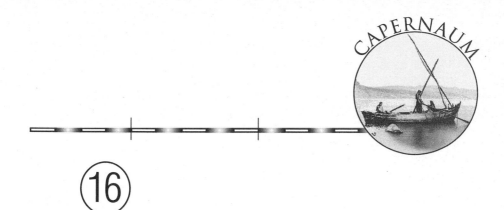

16

CHILDREN IMPORTANT—
the Greatest Spiritual Model

a TEACHING *event*

Reminding adults what it was like to be children was important to Jesus.

JESUS placed great significance on children and our attitude toward them. To Jesus, humble children provide his followers with a model for spiritual learning. A child is trusting and unpretentious.

The love Jesus had for children shows when he instructs his disciples not to rebuke and ignore them. When questioned about who would be the most important in the kingdom of heaven he pointed to the humility and innocence of a child—not to the most influential or knowledgeable or powerful adult.

Jesus also did not want to hinder spiritual learning of children, emphasizing that it was important to allow them to come near to him and participate. He sought to protect children.

For example, those who cause children to sin, Jesus says, face severe punishment. He even says that it would be better for such people to have a millstone hung around their necks and drown.

Finally, Jesus reminds us to receive the kingdom of God like a child: readily, eagerly, with open hearts. Robert H. Schuller, the founder of Crystal Cathedral Ministries, used to say, "Reading the Bible is like eating fish, don't get caught on the bones." Good advice as we study the Bible today! If we cannot catch on to the simple lessons of Jesus, then we will never be ready for the tougher ones. Begin like a child, and keep maintaining the trust and attitude of a child, as well.

Refer to: *Matthew 18:1–9, 19:13–14, Mark 9:33–37*

Questions: Do you remember how you felt about learning when you were a child? Have you felt that way since those days?

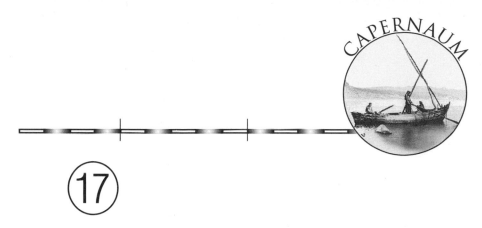

(17)

CONCLUSION OF MINISTRY
IN GALILEE—Transfiguration

an IMPACT *event*

God affirms Jesus, and Jesus sets out resolutely for Jerusalem.

FROM CAESAREA PHILIPPI, Jesus took Peter, James, and John and led them up a mountain. There he was transfigured before their eyes. His face shone like the sun, and his clothes became white with light. He appeared with Moses and Elijah, and the voice of God affirmed Jesus: "This is my Son, whom I have chosen; listen to him" (Luke 9:35b). A similar affirmation from the Father was heard at Jesus's baptism.

As they descended from the mountain Jesus instructed those who were with him not to tell what they had seen until he was raised from the dead. From that time forward Jesus began explaining to his disciples that he must go to Jerusalem,

confront the chief priests, be killed, and on the third day be raised to life. Jesus predicted his betrayal into human hands. The disciples were distressed and did not understand what he was saying.

When they reached Capernaum, on the Sea of Galilee, the collectors of the temple tax came to Peter and asked for Jesus to pay the temple tax. Jesus instructed Peter to go to the sea and take the necessary coin from the mouth of the first fish that he caught in the water. Later he would instruct them to pay to Caesar what is Caesar's and render to God what is God's.

Then Jesus set out for Jerusalem. As his Galilean ministry drew to completion, Jesus had reached and touched people of all backgrounds. He had formed his core group of disciples. And a New Covenant of love had been taught on the foundation of Jewish law and practices.

Refer to: *Matthew 16:21–17:13, Mark 8:31–9:13, Luke 9:28–36*

Questions: Have you ever set out on a journey that you knew would be difficult and challenging? Are you able to see your journey with Christ as a journey—from place to place—in your life?

COME
LIVE

JUDEA / PEREA

After the

Transfiguration

until the

Triumphal Entry

6 Months

7 Events

INTRODUCTION

The last six months of the earthly life of Jesus Christ are a travelog through the provinces of **JUDEA AND PEREA**. These six months represent a turning point in Jesus's life. Some authors call it a period of opposition.

After his receptive audiences in Galilee, "Jesus resolutely set out for Jerusalem" (Luke 9:51b). The stakes for following Jesus are raised. Early in this part of his journey, Jesus warns those who were with him walking along the road: "The Son of Man has no place to lay his head" (Luke 9:58b). He emphasizes a sense of urgency as he says, "Let the dead bury their own dead, but you go and proclaim the kingdom of God" (Luke 9:60b). Again and again in this travelog from Luke (9:51–19:27), Jesus "raises the bar" for his followers.

The base of Jesus's ministry in Judea and Perea was not centered in a particular village. Perea is an area east of Jerusalem across the Jordan River. Jesus received affirmation from God during his travels that would take him twice to feasts in Jerusalem and once to Bethany to raise Lazarus from the dead. In John chapters 7–11 Jesus declares his divinity at the Feast of Tabernacles, the Feast of Dedication, and in raising Lazareth in Bethany. Then, through a series of "I am" claims before Hebrew leaders, he leaves no doubt as to his mission.

Luke is the primary source for this portion of our study and Luke is ordered more by principles than by events. So the events in this section are not necessarily chronological. The Judea/Perea ministry period becomes a time for Jesus to coach his disciples. Values of the kingdom of God and confrontation of Jewish leaders in Jerusalem are also key themes. This section contains seven events—five teaching events and two impact events.

Come Live

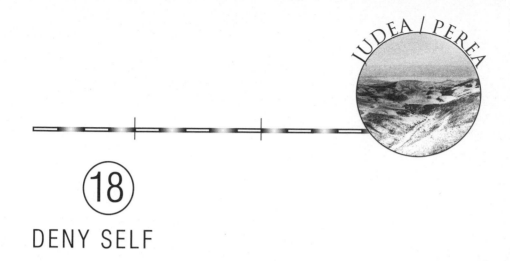

(18)

DENY SELF

a TEACHING *event*

Followers of Jesus are called to be humble.

TOWARD THE END OF THE MINISTRY in Galilee, Jesus told his disciples to keep minimal provisions. "Take nothing for the journey—no staff, no bag, no bread, no money, no extra tunic" (Luke 9:3b). He was beginning to coach his disciples to *deny self* for their emerging responsibilities.

Arguments arose among the disciples as to who would be the greatest. Jesus taught them: "For he who is least among you all—he is the greatest" (Luke 9:48b). Human nature assumes the opposite, to think of self first. Jesus calls his followers to reverse the order; God first, others second, and self last.

Facing Samaritan opposition, Jesus resolutely continued travels toward Jerusalem through other routes (Luke 9:51–53). The disciples suggested bringing down fire from heaven to destroy a village, but Jesus, denying their anger, simply went on to another village. There Jesus encountered a man who volunteered to follow Jesus wherever he would go—after burying his father who had just died. Jesus replied, "Let the dead bury their own dead, but you go and proclaim the kingdom of God" (Luke 9:60). Later, Jesus replied, "No one who puts his hand to the plow and looks back is fit for service in the kingdom of God" (Luke 9:62).

As his travels continue with the disciples, Jesus emphasizes entering through the "narrow door" (Luke 13:24). He is increasingly asking a lot of his followers.

Refer to: *Luke 9, 13, 16:16–31*

Questions: Why do you think it was difficult for the early disciples to fully understand Jesus? When is it difficult for you to follow him as he taught?

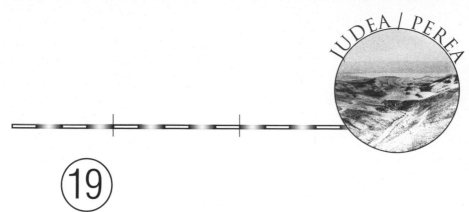

(19)

DECISION WITH FOCUS

a TEACHING *event*

No one can serve two masters.

JESUS reminds the crowds to listen and follow the signs he is giving to them. The Christian journey demands a life completely focused on God. One needs to be completely committed. You have to be "all in."

Jesus tells the Pharisees that although they may clean the outside of their cups, inside they are full of greed and wickedness. Be clean inside! Light the world on the outside. Then in Luke 12 he teaches the values of the kingdom of God. We hear of a rich fool who stored his crops in bigger barns in order to have more for himself, only to lose his life anyway. To be rich toward God requires treasures in heaven, which are more valued than treasures on earth. Jesus reminds us where our

treasure is and says, there your heart should also be. We must be dressed for service and have our lamps burning. Our decision to follow Jesus demands constant focus.

The parable of the shrewd manager (Luke 16:1–15) reminds us that no one can serve two masters. Money is not of great value in God's kingdom. The currency of love from the heart, agape love, is what matters most of all. Zacchaeus, the tax collector, came down from a tree, gave half of his possessions to the poor, and followed Jesus (Luke 19). Jesus uses this as an example of the value of decisiveness and focus!

Refer to: *Luke 11, 12,* and *16:1–15*
Related readings: *Luke 19:1–27*

Question: Do you see any aspect of yourself, and how you might respond under similar circumstances, in the story of Zacchaeus?

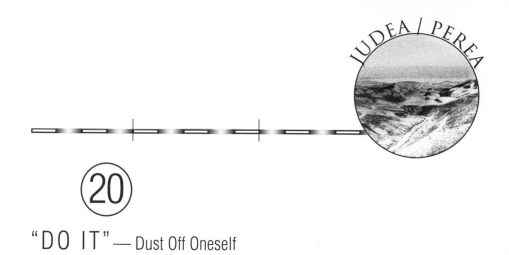

20

"DO IT" — Dust Off Oneself

a TEACHING *event*

Followers of Jesus are given an urgency to serve.

JESUS expects a sense of urgency among his disciples. The old Nike marketing phrase "Just do it" captures this attitude. Jesus wants his followers to jump into the ministry wholeheartedly. A couple of parables demonstrate the importance of taking action and the dangers of not responding to God's call.

In the story of the Good Samaritan (Luke 10:25–37) an expert on the law approaches Jesus and asks what he might do to inherit eternal life. Jesus asks him how he reads the law and the expert responds, "Love the Lord . . . and love your neighbor." Jesus compliments him for knowing this much. The

expert then asks, "Who is my neighbor?" and Jesus responds by telling the man the parable of the Good Samaritan. A priest, a Levite, and a Samaritan passed a man who had been beaten and was in need of care. The priest and the Levite (respected men in the Jewish community) passed by without giving him help. Only the Samaritan, a person looked down upon at the time, took pity on the man and took care of him. Jesus asks the expert which was the good neighbor (a Samaritan?) and concludes by saying, "Go and do likewise" (Luke 10:37b).

In the parable of the Great Banquet (Luke 14:15–24) Jesus tells of a certain man who was preparing a great banquet. Although he asked many guests to attend, most had excuses and could not come. The question Jesus asks is, if God is the one preparing that banquet and inviting us, who will come? Who will accept the invitation?

Refer to: *Luke 10, 14,* and *15*

Question: Do you see yourself in either of the parables that Jesus told in this event?

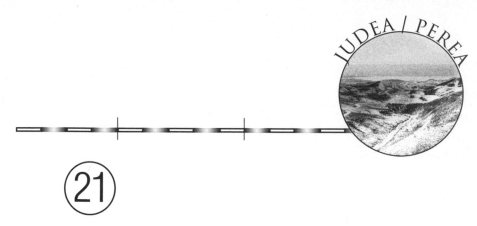

21

DWELLING WITH HIM DAILY

a TEACHING *event*

The richness of a relationship with Jesus has great value.

NEAR the conclusion of the Judea/Perea ministry, Jesus began predicting his death to his disciples. He also laid groundwork for the indwelling power of the Holy Spirit that would soon be available to his followers. And he warns his disciples, "Things that cause people to sin are bound to come . . . so watch yourselves" (Luke 17:1–3).

After Pharisees asked Jesus when the kingdom of God would come, he replied, "The kingdom of God does not come with your careful observation, nor will people say, 'Here it is,' or 'There it is,' because the kingdom of God is within you" (Luke 17:20–21). Followers of Jesus are people dwelling with his spirit in their hearts.

When Peter expresses the concern of the disciples and the plight of Jesus's followers in Luke 18:28, "We have left all we had to follow you," Jesus again predicts his death and resurrection (Luke 18:31–34). Jesus promises his disciples they will receive much more in the age to come: *eternal life.* We are told, however, that the disciples did not understand this message.

Author Brian D. McLaren offers this thought in his 2001 book, *A New Kind of Christian*: "The lowest available risk that I see is the risk of journeying on in faith. You see, I believe in the Holy Spirit. I believe Jesus meant it when he said the Spirit of God would be with us, guiding us, to the very end. So I believe that he will guide us through the winds and currents of change, no matter what storms come. In fact, I believe that he is the wind in our sails, leading us into the change, because that's his way."

Refer to: *Luke 17* and *18*

Questions: Why do you think the early disciples had trouble understanding or believing Jesus's teachings about the future? Do you have similar difficulties?

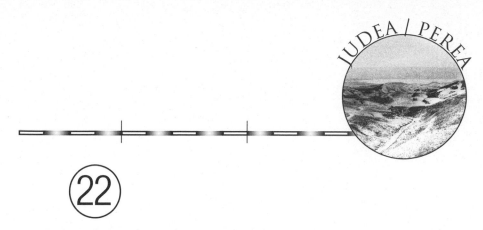

22

DISCOURAGE DIVORCE

a TEACHING *event*

Value a good marriage! Two becoming one is to be cherished.

A GROUP OF PHARISEES came to Jesus with a difficult question concerning divorce. "Is it lawful for a man to divorce his wife for any and every reason?" (Matthew 19:3b). For his answer Jesus went back to the original purpose of marriage in Genesis 1:27 and 2:24, when God created man and woman in his own image and in marriage two become one flesh. Jesus then discourages divorce by saying, "So they are no longer two, but one. Therefore what God has joined together, let man not separate" (Matthew 19:6).

Again and again, Jesus does not focus on laws, but on where the heart is.

This is the goal in marriage: two become one. When the love of Christ and his Cross are at the center of a marriage relationship, this is the beginning of God's vision of two becoming one—in him.

Likewise, the message for today is clear: Center your marriage on Christ, and pray always together. Marriage partners who pray together, stay together!

Refer to: *Matthew 19:1–12, Mark 10:1–12*
Related readings: *Genesis 1:27 and 2:24*

Questions: How is the marriage relationship similar to a relationship with God? When is it different?

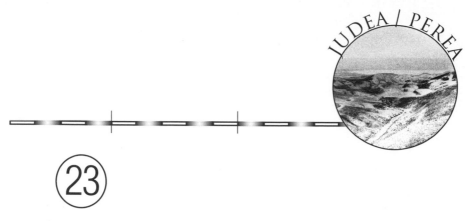

(23)

DIGNITY OF WOMEN

IMPACT *events*

The ground is level at the foot of the Cross.

THROUGHOUT HIS MINISTRY Jesus elevated women and demonstrated their dignity in ways that were surprising to his contemporaries. Now that Jesus was on the move from place to place, women continued to play an important role tending to his needs and those of his disciples.

Early in his ministry, he honored his mother's concerns with a first miracle, changing water into wine at a wedding in Cana (John 2). His dialog with a Samaritan woman at the well in Sychar (John 4) again showed respect for a woman in his early ministry. In John 11:5, we see the love that Jesus had for Martha, her sister Mary, and Lazarus. Later in the Gospel narratives, women are the first at the tomb to see the risen

Christ. Many experiences such as these illustrate the importance women played in the life of Jesus.

Here is a list of stories and events from the four Gospels that are worth closer study.

EVENT	PASSAGE
Mary and Martha—Lazarus healed	John 11
Mary chosen as the Mother of Jesus	Matthew 1:18–25
All women, adultery defined	Matthew 5:27–30
Canaanite mother, daughter healed	Matthew 15:21–28
Bleeding woman healed	Mark 5:25–34
Daughter of Jarius healed	Mark 5:21–24, 35–43
Poor widow recognized	Mark 12:41–44
Woman who anoints Jesus is appreciated	Luke 7:36–50
Widow of Nain, dead son healed	Luke 7:7–17
Crippled woman healed on the Sabbath	Luke 13:10–17
Samaritan woman becomes evangelist	John 4:1–26
Woman caught in adultery forgiven	John 8:1–11
Women last at the cross	Luke 23:49
Mary Magdalene first at empty tomb of Jesus	John 20:10–18

Question: Jesus went out of his way to show respect for women in his own day, contrary to the norms of his era. What groups of people need that sort of respect from us today?

(24)

DIVINITY DECLARED

an IMPACT event

Jesus teaches that he and the Father are one.

DURING THE JUDEA/PEREA travels Jesus made two trips to the Jerusalem Temple and one trip to Bethany, near Jerusalem. Jesus went to the Temple for the Feast of the Tabernacles (John 7:1–10:21) and to the Feast of Dedication (John 10:22–42). During these Jerusalem travels, one can detect the challenges and barriers Jesus faced with the entrenched Jewish leaders in Jerusalem.

The Gospel of John records an important step in Jesus's ministry at this time. With his "I am" statements, Jesus openly declares his divinity directly to Temple leaders. We can learn a lot from these. Below is a summary guide to all of Jesus's "I am" claims from John's Gospel:

JOHN	"I AM" STATEMENTS
7:16	"My teaching is not my own. It comes from him who sent me."
7:28	"I am not here on my own, but he who sent me is true."
7:33	"I am with you for only a short time, and then I go to the one who sent me."
8:12	"I am the light of the world."
8:16	"I am not alone. I stand with the Father, who sent me."
8:23–24	"I am from above. . . . I am not of this world."
8:49	"I am not possessed by a demon."
8:50	"I am not seeking glory for myself."
8:58	"Before Abraham was born, I am!"
10:7	"I am the gate for the sheep."
10:11–15	"I am the good shepherd . . . and I lay down my life for the sheep."
10:14	"I am the good shepherd; I know my sheep and my sheep know me."
10:30	"I and the Father are one."
11:25	"I am the resurrection and the life."

The Jewish leaders continued to build their case against Jesus. "'We are not stoning you for any of these,' replied the Jews, 'but for blasphemy, because you, a mere man, claim to be God'" (John 10:33). Jesus does not back down and concludes, "Understand that the Father is in me, and I in the Father" (John 10:38b).

John 11 records the visit of Jesus to Bethany, to Mary and Martha, and to raise their brother Lazarus from the dead. Jesus shares with Martha, "I am the resurrection and the life. He who believes in me will live, even though he dies" (John 11:25b). Later, Jesus called in a loud voice, "Lazarus come out!" (John 11:43b) and the dead man, Lazarus, came out of his tomb!

Refer to: *John 7–11*

Questions: What do you think of the bold "I am" claims Jesus made? How do they relate to the meaning of your own Christian faith?

COME
HOME

JERUSALEM

The most

important week,

the Passion

to Pentecost

7 + 50 Days

8 Events

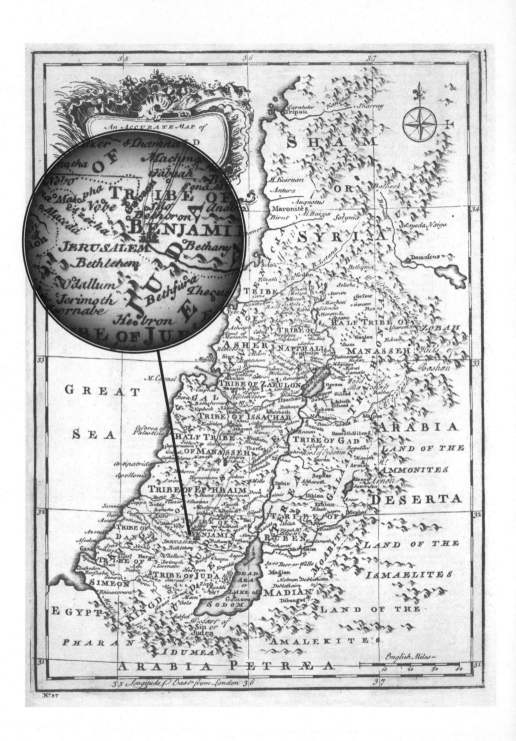

INTRODUCTION

Events in **JERUSALEM** cover the seven-day Passover period, Jesus's resurrection experiences through his ascension (forty days), and the power of the Holy Spirit being with the apostles at Pentecost (fifty days after Passover). We will walk with Jesus during the last days of his earthly ministry and experience the grief of the Cross and joy of the Resurrection on Easter Sunday.

We will see his disciples with the power of the Holy Spirit on the day of Pentecost. About thirty-five percent of all of the material that makes up the four Gospels of the New Testament are devoted to these last days in Jerusalem. Each of the Gospel writers addresses a different audience in their writing, but all assign great importance to reporting the events of this period.

There are eight event studies among these Jerusalem travels. Three are impact events, three are teaching events, and two are God events.

What unifies the four Gospels in their telling of these events are the stories of the empty tomb and the power of the risen Christ. It is here that Jesus left the ministry of the Word with his disciples, calling them to become *apostles* of the faith. He had no other plan then . . . and he has no other plan today. The faith is left in the hands, heads, and hearts of his followers to be his witnesses to the ends of the earth.

Come Home

TRIUMPHAL ENTRY

an IMPACT *event*

Crowds shout "Hosanna!" as Jesus enters Jerusalem.

A S THEY APPROACHED JERUSALEM, Jesus instructed two of his disciples to go on ahead, where they would find a donkey with her colt. The disciples brought the donkey and the colt and placed cloaks on their backs, and Jesus sat upon the colt. According to Matthew 21, large crowds went ahead of him shouting, "Hosanna to the Son of David." As Jesus entered Jerusalem, the whole city was stirred and asked, "Who is this?" The crowd answered, "This is Jesus, the prophet from Nazareth in Galilee."

John actually begins his account of the Triumphal Entry event the evening before (chapter 12). Here, Jesus is enjoying a dinner with Mary, Martha, and Lazarus. Mary anoints Jesus's feet with costly pure nard, a perfume. Judas, who is also there,

questions her actions. Jesus affirms Mary's actions and talks of his day of burial. Jesus notes, "You will always have the poor among you, but you will not always have me." Anticipation is building.

It is interesting to compare the accounts of Jesus's arrival into Jerusalem with the arrival the Jews expected of a messiah. Many Jews living when Jesus came were looking for another leader, a king who would save them from the oppression of the Romans. Nearly 1,000 years before, David and his mighty men had conquered the Philistines and the surrounding tribes. Jews thought surely God would send another leader to remove the yoke of Roman domination and restore the golden age. *God had a different plan!* The Messiah would be a servant instead. He would suffer death on a cross. Jesus was a suffering servant. The Old Testament foretold this Messiah, as it turns out, and a look at Isaiah 52:13–53:12 confirms this. The triumphal entry was the fulfillment of this prophecy.

Refer to: *Matthew 21:1–11, Mark 11:1–11, Luke 19:28–44, John 12:1–19*

Question: Can you appreciate the fact that Jesus led no armed forces and was not a national king or leader, but his life is the hinge of human history and changed the world forever?

(26)

TEMPLE CLEARED FOR PRAYER

an IMPACT *event*

Monday of Passion Week

Jesus clears the Temple and points to a withered fig tree as a symbol of dried-up faith.

FOLLOWING THE TRIUMPHAL ENTRY, Jesus returns to Bethany. The next day Jesus returns to the Temple to cast out the money changers and to cleanse the Temple as a house of prayer for all people. Think of the change in ambience and attitudes Jesus created by cleansing the Temple. He was beginning to confront the religious leaders, revealing more and more of the New Covenant. After the Hosannas and celebration of the previous day, Jesus showed more of the values of the kingdom of God.

On the way to the Temple on that Monday morning, Jesus said to a fig tree, "May no one ever eat fruit from you again"

(Mark 11:14). The disciples found the fig tree withered the next morning on their way to the Temple. Fig trees normally grow leaves in March and April but do not produce fruit until June when their leaves are full. This tree was an exception. At Passover time it was already full of leaves yet had no fruit. This odd incident provides a parable on the religion of the Temple and its lack of fruit. It is a visual symbol for Jesus to use as he returns to the Temple on Tuesday and challenges the Temple leadership regarding the fruitlessness of their faith.

Refer to: Matthew 21:12–22
Mark 11:12–25
Luke 19:45–48

Questions: Is there any temple clearing needed in our churches today? What might "clearing the temple" mean on a personal level, in your own life?

TEACHING IN THE TEMPLE

a TEACHING *event*

Tuesday of Passion Week

Jesus has one last teaching opportunity with Temple leaders.

THE CHIEF PRIESTS and elders came to question Jesus in the Temple, asking where his authority derived from. Initially, Jesus did not tell them by what authority he was doing miracles and teaching. Instead, he indicated that the kingdom of God was more important than religious leadership and that the kingdom would be given to people who will produce fruit.

As Jesus silenced the Sadducees, the Pharisees got together and asked, "Teacher, which is the greatest commandment of the Law?" Jewish Law consisted of more than 600 rabbinical teachings. Jesus's reply was simple: "'Love the Lord your God with all your heart and with all your soul and with all your

mind.' This is the first and greatest commandment. And the second is like it: 'Love your neighbor as yourself.' All the Law and the Prophets hang on these two commandments" (Matthew 22:37–40).

In Matthew 23 Jesus went on to point out the hypocrisy of the teachers of the law and the Pharisees by saying "they do not practice what they preach" (Matthew 23:3b). He lists seven woes that scribes and Pharisees used to shut out the kingdom of heaven to other people: devouring widow's houses; instructing proselytes poorly; swearing oaths that mean nothing to God in heaven; avoiding weightier matters (judgment, mercy, and faith); preaching excess; being beautiful outside while dead inside; and killing and crucifying their prophets.

Refer to: *Matthew 21:18–23:39*
Mark 11:20–12:44
Luke 20:1–21:4
John 12:20–50

Questions: What might happen in the world if we taught Jesus's simple message to love our neighbor and love God? What might be the "seven woes" that we use to shut out the kingdom of heaven today?

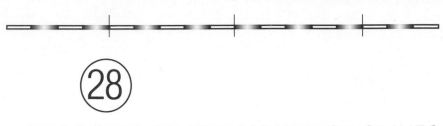

TEACHING ON THE MOUNT OF OLIVES

a TEACHING *event*

Tuesday evening of Passion Week

Jesus on the Mount of Olives teaches his disciples regarding the end times and judgment.

JESUS and his disciples leave the Temple area and retreat to the Mount of Olives, across the Kidron Valley. In Matthew 24, the disciples ask about the end of the age. Jesus answers them, "This gospel of the kingdom will be preached in the whole world as a testimony to all nations, and then the end will come" (Matthew 24:14). Jesus then shares about the endurance of the Word, "Heaven and earth will pass away, but my words will never pass away" (Matthew 24:35).

He goes on to tell them that the day and hour of his return is known by no one, not even the Son, only the Father. (Hard to fathom—no wonder the disciples often failed to understand!)

Finally, in Matthew 25, Jesus tells three parables to conclude his thoughts on the signs of his coming and the end of the age. These are known as:

- The Parable of the Ten Virgins.
- The Parable of the Talents.
- The Parable of the Sheep and the Goats.

Through these parables—three of the most famous ones in all of Scripture—Jesus teaches the importance of preparedness, of using our talents for God's service, and the reward that comes to those who serve those in need.

Refer to: *Matthew 24 and 25, Mark 13, Luke 21:5-38*

Questions: Look closely at those parables in the Gospel of Matthew and consider: Is Jesus's message one that is important for your life today? How?

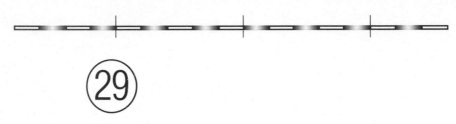

(29)

TIME HAD COME—Upper Room to Gethsemane

a TEACHING *event*

From Wednesday evening to Thursday of Passion Week
Jesus shares last words with his disciples.

JESUS knew the *time had come* for him to leave this world and go to the Father. It was time to share his final moments with his disciples.

In these moments we glimpse Jesus showing his disciples the full extent of his love. Pouring water into a basin, he washed their feet. Foot washing was a custom of the times. Feet with sandals were both tired and dirty at the end of a day. But it was unheard of for the leader or rabbi to do this sort of work for his followers. Not so for Jesus. He showed them that hospitality, warmth, and equality were all a servant's task, that he was a servant, and that they were all called to be servants

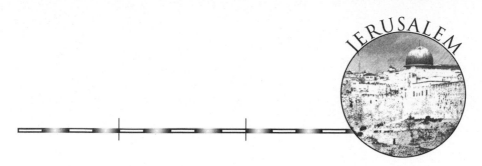

for God. Jesus called his followers to action: "Now that you know these things, you will be blessed if you do them" (John 13:17).

Jesus then comforts his followers by telling them that he is going to prepare a place for them (John 14:1–4). The way of serving will not be easy; Peter will betray his calling three times very shortly thereafter. But Jesus leaves us a counselor, the Holy Spirit, to be with us forever.

The bread (body) and wine (blood) that Jesus shares in the Upper Room become a cleansing celebration of his life. As they take leave of the Upper Room, Jesus tells them: "I am the true vine, and my Father is the gardener. . . . You are the branches. If a man remains in me and I in him, he will bear much fruit" (John 15:1–5). He also commands them to "Love each other" (John 15:17b).

Jesus completes this intimate discourse with his disciples in prayer to the Father (John 17). "I have made you known to them, . . . in order that the love you have for me may be in them" (John 17:26). How ironic (and how human) it is that when Jesus finished praying for his disciples and caring for them in these intimate ways, they had crossed the Kidron Valley to the Gethsemane garden and, despite Jesus's asking them to remain with him, his disciples fell asleep! It is then

and there that Jesus prayed to the Father: "Father, if you are willing, take this cup from me; yet not my will, but yours be done" (Luke 22:42).

Refer to: Matt. 26:1–46
Mark 14:1–42
Luke 22:1–46
John 13:1–17:26

Questions: What do you think of servant leadership? Does it work? How do we "remain" in Jesus today (see John 15:5)?

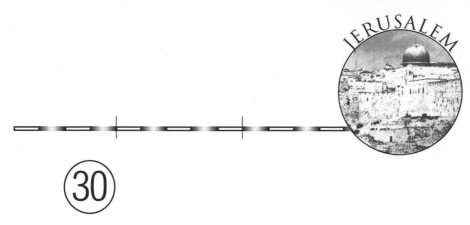

(30)

TRIALS, ARREST, CRUCIFIXION, AND DEATH

an IMPACT *event*

From Thursday evening to Friday of Passion Week
The trials and subsequent death of Jesus on the cross.

JUDAS guided soldiers to arrest Jesus in the Garden of Gethsemane. Jesus's trials then begin as he is first taken to Annas, the father-in-law of Caiaphas, the high priest, and then to Caiaphas himself. It is in the courtyard while Jesus is before the high priest that Peter famously denies knowing Jesus three times. Then Jesus was transferred to Pontius Pilate, who asked Jesus if he was the king of the Jews. Jesus states that those are Pilate's words, not his, and that his kingdom is not of this world.

Frustrated, Pilate has Jesus flogged and again questions him. Finding nothing criminally wrong, Pilate leaves the

decision of his fate to the mass of people who are gathered outside. They insist that Jesus be crucified. Pilate approves the crucifixion and Roman soldiers take charge of Jesus. Fulfilling Old Testament Scripture (Psalm 22), soldiers cast lots for his clothing and do not break his legs, which was the custom. In a beautiful moment upon the cross, Jesus, a compassionate son, turns to direct the care of his mother to his disciple and friend John (John 19:25–27).

The sacrifice God the Father and his Son Jesus made on the cross shows their love for all people. As it says in John 15:13, "Greater love has no one than this, that he lay down his life for his friends."

Jesus said from the cross: "Father, forgive them, for they do not know what they are doing" (Luke 23:34a). When the Word became flesh and dwelt among us 2,000 years ago, Jesus was rejected. We today stand at the foot of the cross and survey it with awe. God's love and Jesus's forgiveness are for all people.

Refer to: *Matthew 26:47–27:66*
Mark 14:43–15:47
Luke 22:47–23:56
John 18:1–19:42

Questions: Can you understand how Jesus would give his life on the cross for the forgiveness of our sins? How would you describe the relationship between the Son and the Father?

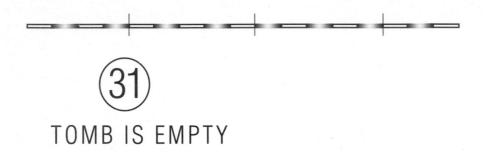

31

TOMB IS EMPTY

a GOD *event*

Sunday of Passion Week (Easter)
Christ our Lord has risen today!

A FTER RESTING on the Sabbath, early on the first day of the week, while it was still dark, some women returned to the tomb with spices. Mary Magdalene first saw that the stone had been removed. She stood outside the tomb, crying. Then a man, who she thought was the gardener, approached. He asked, "Who is it you are looking for?" She explained she couldn't find the body of Jesus. Jesus caught her eye and said her name, "Mary." She turned and cried out, "Rabboni!" (John 20:15–16).

Meanwhile, the disciples were together in the Upper Room. The door was locked for fear of the religious leaders. Jesus came and stood among them. But one of the disciples, Thomas,

was not present at this first appearance of Jesus to his disciples. John 20 concludes as Thomas states, "Unless I see the nail marks in his hands and put my finger where the nails were, and put my hand into his side, I will not believe it" (John 20:25). A week later Jesus appears again to the disciples and Thomas was there. Jesus told him to stop doubting. Thomas answered, "My Lord and my God!" (John 20:28b). Jesus said, "Because you have seen me, you have believed; blessed are those who have not seen and yet have believed" (John 20:29).

Over a forty-day period Jesus appeared to the disciples and others. He spoke about the kingdom of God. On one occasion he gave a command, "Do not leave Jerusalem . . . you will be baptized by the Holy Spirit" (Acts 1:4–5).

Refer to: *Matthew 28, Mark 16, Luke 24, John 20–21, Acts 9:1–19*

Questions: What do you think of Thomas, who is often called "Doubting Thomas"? What do you think of Mary Magdalene—what sort of faith did she have?

(32)

TEACH AND TALK—Be My Witnesses

a GOD *event*

The risen Christ leaves instructions for his followers.

IN GALILEE, Jesus appeared to his eleven disciples. He instructed them: "Therefore go and make disciples of all nations, baptizing them in the name of the Father and of the Son and of the Holy Spirit, and teaching them to obey everything I have commanded you. And surely I am with you always, to the very end of the age" (Matthew 28:19–20). This is known as the "Great Commission," when Jesus instructed his followers to evangelize and teach the truth of Jesus and God's Word.

Later on the Mount of Olives in Jerusalem, at the Ascension, he said to those assembled: "But you will receive power when the Holy Spirit comes on you; and you will be my witnesses in Jerusalem, and in all Judea and Samaria, and to the ends of the earth" (Acts 1:8). Followers of Jesus are empowered by this incredible gift, the Spirit of God, to be his witnesses. This is how we are able to talk of Jesus, his divine nature, his impact on lives today, and to invite people to follow him.

Jesus Christ was taken up before their very eyes, and a cloud hid him from their sight. The remaining eleven disciples (Judas had defected and died) then joined together in prayer with the women, including Mary the mother of Jesus. Later, all of the apostles met in Jerusalem and affirmed the call of Jesus to Gentiles (non-Jewish people), to all the people of the world (Acts 15).

Refer to: *Matthew 28:16–20, Acts 1, 2, and 15, 1 Corinthians 15:5–11*

Questions: Have you ever felt spiritual power? Where did it come from? What does God want from you and from your life?

CONCLUSION

In the Upper Room, Jesus shared instructions with his disciples. He noted, "You call me 'Teacher' and 'Lord,' and rightly so" (John 13:13). Then he set an example of service by washing his disciples' feet. He told them: "Now that you know these things, you will be blessed if you do them" (John 13:17).

If you do them. We all want lives of blessing. Jesus tells us how to be blessed: by doing the things he called us to do.

I have learned much in writing this short guide to the life of Jesus. I am called to do something with my knowledge. We live in a world that needs *more of Jesus*. His love, compassion, truth, and forgiveness are needed in our lives, marriages, families, communities, churches, nations, and the whole world. Jesus tells us the blessings that will come when we do what he asks of us. There is joy in doing!

So, consider what you will do. This book may call you to be a better follower of Jesus, or to be prepared to share his life in spiritual dialog with others. The apostle Peter reminds us, "Always be prepared to give an answer to everyone who asks you to give the reason for the hope that you have. But do this with gentleness and respect" (1 Peter 3:15b).

For those who are not followers of Jesus, what questions did these thirty-two events leave in your mind? Are you interested in learning more? Find a local church, community, or friend who is a follower of Jesus. Ask questions and observe the community of those who follow him. Presumably they will not disappoint you! Consider answering the call of Jesus, "Come follow me."

Each of us learns in different ways. How we share Christ's story and our story is unique and different.

Engaging in spiritual dialog is not easy. When meeting or dialoging with someone, I try to learn first the other person's spiritual journey. I try to listen as others explain their spiritual journeys. I don't have all the answers; thus I want to be inclusive and learn from others (rather than "exclusive"—as if I've got all the answers). Only then have I earned the right to share my spiritual journey and faith with people. If we are about changing the outcomes in our families, society, and world today, I believe a Christ-centered, Spirit-filled dialog is a good starting point. My greatest hope for *A Biography of Jesus* is that it will cause people to listen and talk with others about their journey with Christ and what that can mean for the world around them.

Early in my journey with Jesus I liked the "bloom where you are planted" example and challenge. We are placed in his kingdom at this time with a purpose and a calling. As you review your notes from this study, what are the next steps you are called to prayerfully consider and act upon? Do you want to better understand the Jesus you have discovered here? Given who you uniquely are, what systems or approaches is Jesus calling you to use to serve with him? Whatever those things are, let's do them—all of us.

THE LAND OF JESUS

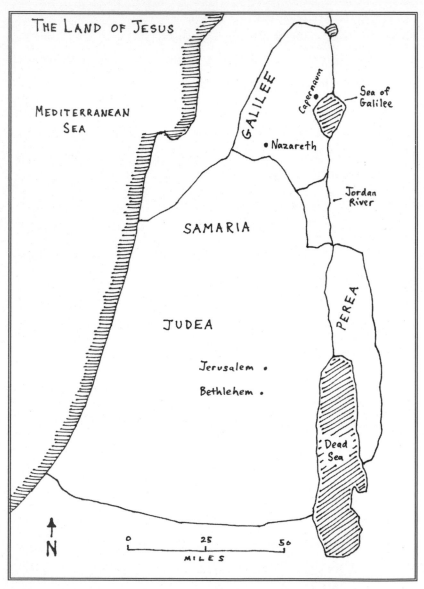

Map by Robbie Collins

JERUSALEM AT THE TIME OF JESUS

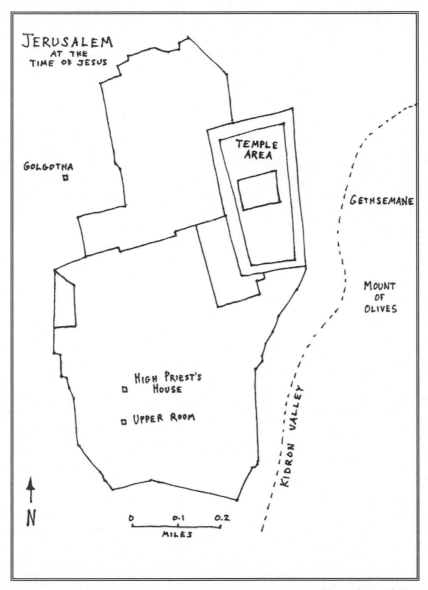

Map by Robbie Collins

ABOUT PARACLETE PRESS

Who We Are

Paraclete Press is a publisher of books, recordings, and DVDs on Christian spirituality. Our publishing represents a full expression of Christian belief and practice—from Catholic to Evangelical, from Protestant to Orthodox. We are the publishing arm of the Community of Jesus, an ecumenical monastic community in the Benedictine tradition. As such, we are uniquely positioned in the marketplace without connection to a large corporation and with informal relationships to many branches and denominations of faith.

What We Are Doing

Books Paraclete publishes books that show the richness and depth of what it means to be Christian. Although Benedictine spirituality is at the heart of all that we do, we publish books that reflect the Christian experience across many cultures, time periods, and houses of worship. We publish books that nourish the vibrant life of the church and its people— books about spiritual practice, formation, history, ideas, and customs.

We have several different series, including the best-selling Paraclete Essentials and Paraclete Giants series of classic texts in contemporary English; A Voice from the Monastery—men and women monastics writing about living a spiritual life today; award-winning poetry; best-selling gift books for children on the occasions of baptism and first communion; and the Active Prayer Series that brings creativity and liveliness to any life of prayer.

Recordings From Gregorian chant to contemporary American choral works, our music recordings celebrate sacred choral music through the centuries. Paraclete distributes the recordings of the internationally acclaimed choir Gloriæ Dei Cantores, praised for their "rapt and fathomless spiritual intensity" by *American Record Guide,* and the Gloriæ Dei Cantores Schola, which specializes in the study and performance of Gregorian chant. Paraclete is also the exclusive North American distributor of the recordings of the Monastic Choir of St. Peter's Abbey in Solesmes, France, long considered to be a leading authority on Gregorian chant.

Videos Our videos offer spiritual help, healing, and biblical guidance for life issues: grief and loss, marriage, forgiveness, anger management, facing death, and spiritual formation.

Learn more about us at our website:
www.paracletepress.com, or call us toll-free at 1-800-451-5006.

SCAN
TO
READ
MORE

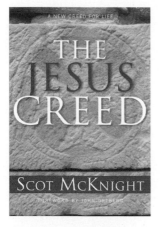
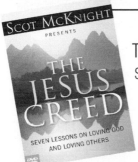
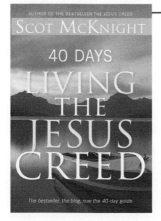

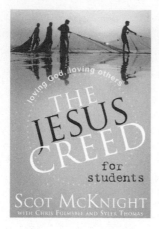